My Glasses Are Off

How Love Will Draw

By

Michael McMillon

My Glasses Are Off – How Love Will Draw

Edited by: Lora Mitchell
Published by: McMillon Publications

Scripture quotations marked MSG or The Message are taken from The Holy Bible, The Message. Copyright© 1993, 1994, 1995, 1996, 2000, 2001, 2002 by NavPress Publishing Group. Used by permission. All rights reserved.

Scripture quotations, marked NLT are taken from The Holy Bible, New Living Translation, Copyright© 1996. Used by permission of Tyndale House Publishers, Inc., Wheaton, Illinois 60189. All rights reserved.

For information on getting permission for reprints and excerpts, contact: michaelmcmillon.com

Table of Contents

Introduction

1

When I was 13 years old, the song titled "Love" was released by Muisq Soulchild. Cool name… I know, right. The song was a hit. There have been over 900 songs with love in the title since 1960.

"Endless Love" by Diana Ross & Lionel Richie, August 1981.
"Greatest Love of All" by Whitney Houston, May 1986.
"I Want to Know What Love Is" by Foreigner, January 1985.

In the beginning, I believe humanity was trying to figure out what love is. I have always viewed love as an emotion. That is what I grew up hearing. I later changed my view when I heard a Pastor, Michael Hayes while ministering in a particular service as he pointed out that "love is not an emotion, it is a person." Immediately the scripture in 1 John 4:8 came to my mind, which states, God is love. I would not have known that scripture if it was not for one of my mentors, Michael Kelley. Yes, now you see why Michael is an awesome name. (Haha) Michael taught me about the Father's love for us and spiritual practices such as worship and praying in tongues.

A little story about me is that I grew up in a Christian home with my parents, Willie McMillon, and Maria McMillon, who became Pastors of Fair Temple C.O.G.I.C when I was seven years old. It was a miraculous story seeing as my father was a sailor from Cleveland, Ohio, who met my mom in a McDonald's in Virginia Beach, Virginia. Later, they would marry and have kids in Cleveland, Ohio. They were young, trying to follow God's heart, leading people while raising us.

At that time, we were a part of an organization with good music, strict teachings, tuned-up Preaching, and a lot of shouting and dancing. In my youth, I spent more time asking God to forgive me every second of the day because that was the direction the teachings led me. It was not until I started spending more time with God and surrounding myself with other believers that I began to change my perspective. I realized how much God loved me. I learned my purpose and started walking in that purpose. I noticed people become afraid of God instead of drawing closer to him. They unintentionally distance themselves from Him, not realizing that it was fear keeping them away. Part of my purpose was to help those in my shoes and provide them with the knowledge I learned.

For example, if you are afraid of snakes and spiders, how often will you be around them? Will you want to be in their presence? It does not matter if someone said you need this spider or snake in your life. You would stay away, ignoring the person. What happens when you are afraid of God - you find yourself not talking to him (prayer), not as close and intimate with him, and you find yourself avoiding him. I was one of those people who were afraid of God. I looked at God as the Father - the mean one, Jesus was the nice one, and the Holy Spirit was the mediator. I did not realize it was God, the Father's idea to save the world through His son because He loves us (John 3:16 NIV).

Being a Pastor's kid, I went to every bible study and every Sunday School. I am grateful because I learned some cool bible stories as a kid. I was able to act out stories in a play, thanks to my auntie, Matilda Day. She was certainly one of the best Sunday school teachers we had. Matilda was very relatable yet knowledgeable. Even with my parents being Pastors and learning from different bible teachers such as my grandmother, participating in plays, and even singing in the choir, I still did not know God. Thank God for Phillip, a disciple of Jesus who asked an important question. He asked, "Lord, show us the Father, and we will be satisfied." (John 14:8 NLT) If I heard him ask that question, I would say, "Yes, Phillip! Good question. I have wanted to know that answer as well."

Look what Jesus says to Phillip: "Have I been with you all this time, Phillip, and yet you still don't know who I am? Anyone who has seen me has seen the Father. So why are you asking me to show him to you?" (John 14:9 NIV) What Jesus was trying to do was help Phillip and the world to see Jesus' character, His heart, the compassion, and the love that He has shown. Jesus showed mercy as well as forgiveness. He took care of the needs of the people, the times He ate and spent intimate time with the considered outcast tax collectors and known offenders, or the people with leprosy banished from their land - whom Jesus healed and restored. The times Jesus healed all manner of sickness and diseases. The times He cared about the broken-hearted and made it known people could "cast their cares upon him." Jesus did all of this because God, the Father, wanted it. Jesus made it known that He only did what He saw the Father doing. So, when we see Jesus, we see the Father.

Therefore, we can know God the Father. We can be like Jesus and talk to the Father often to know His heart. Did Jesus have the old scrolls? Yes, but He never let that replace intimate time with the Father. And I would encourage you not to replace personal time with the Father by only reading the Bible. I can read about God, hear about Him, but that does not mean I know Him personally. For example, I have read stories and watched movies about Martin Luther King Jr.

I've also heard people talk about him, but I've never met him, nor have I spent time in his presence. As a result, I cannot tell if the things I heard or read about him are true.

In John 17:3 NLT, Jesus says to the Pharisees, "You search the Scriptures because you think they give you eternal life, but the scriptures point to me!" What did Jesus want to show the Pharisees? Basically everyone? That you can know him personally, to get in his presence, to see His character. Imagine if your spouse comes home, "Honey, I'm home, what are you doing?" and then you say, "Nothing, honey, just reading this book about you." Your spouse will then say, "Ok, honey, that's nice, but I thought we could spend some intimate time together." Imagine you saying, "No, babe, I'd rather read this book about you." Your spouse would say, "Honey, you know I'm right here. You know that book is talking about me, the one right here in your face? Anything you want to know; I can tell you. Just spend time with me."

You see how much your spouse wanted intimacy with you. Was the book helpful? Yes. Can you learn some things? Yes, but imagine what you can learn in that intimate place with your spouse where no one else is allowed. This is what God desires with you: an intimate time where He can show you His ways, His heart, His plan for you.

The Bible is good; you can learn some powerful lessons and hear great testimonies, but what is God saying to you? What is your testimony? What work is He performing or working through you? Many in the scriptures have found salvation and shared their stories.

Now it is your turn, your time to share what you have heard and learned by being in God's presence.

Did you ever find yourself afraid of God?
(And no, I'm not referring to reverence and respect

Do you spend intimate time with God? How often?

NOTES

Experiencing the Love of God

2

The only time I would hear about Jesus loving us was listening to the song "Jesus loves me, this I know, for the Bible tells me so." I grew up hearing more about how we should love God. I did not know that John 4:10 existed: "This is real love - not that we loved God, but that he loved us." Our focus needs to be on God's Love for us. God didn't leave me in that state, and this is because of his goodness and kindness. He began to orchestrate events and place people in my life that would help prepare me for my destiny.

At first, it was not completely clear to me, but my family was a huge factor in shaping my destiny. My brothers, Willie, Marc, and David McMillon and I started a singing group and added my best friend, Reginald Bowens, and later my cousin Christopher Merritt. The group currently only consists of my brothers and cousin. Our group, Nu Covenant, would sing at numerous places around the country. We were singing gospel music, but we never spent any personal time with God to get to know Him. When we released our first album, we received opportunities to perform at a lot of places. We enjoyed performing and putting on a show! Our dance moves were a hit! The funny thing is, I always wanted to be a choreographer. I would teach our group dance moves. We often stayed away from slow-tempo songs because they were not easy to choreograph. Our group was invited to a festival in Ashtabula, Ohio, where we sang and danced. A choir was also there to sing, but they did not have musicians, so my brother, Willie, walked on stage and played the piano while I played the drums.

After the concert, a lady named Latonya Jackson approached me about attending a workshop. She asked if I could play the drums. Now I love drums, so I immediately said yes, not knowing that this

15

lady would later become my Godmother. She taught me about the importance of intimate worship. I remember a song would end, and she would not move on. She would want me to swell the cymbals softly while the piano player plays beautiful chords. The choir would have their eyes closed and some with their hands raised. Now I was not used to this - remember, I stayed away from slow gospel songs. I only wanted to play fast up-tempo songs that make you clap or dance. Worshipping God in this way was different. It is almost like seeing a couple hold hands for the first time in your life. It is interesting but weird at the same time. When I would sing or play, it was not because I focused on using my gifts to display the Love of God. I played because of the love I had for music.

I did not know at the time that everything we do helps show the Glory of God. I did not know that God wants to be intimate with us. He wants to spend time with us; God wants to speak to us. He desires us. He is a loving Father who wants to express that love to us. It is like meeting someone with all the attributes you want in a spouse and you desiring to have a relationship with them, and they make it known that they have wanted a relationship with you since the first time they laid eyes on you. You will feel special, why? Because what you have been desiring and looking for, you have finally found. And to know they want to take care of you, or be with you, or spend time with you, and enter a place of intimacy where you know them, and they know you. That is the joy of being intimate with God. You have someone all-knowing, all-powerful, a provider, a healer, a way maker, and a protector that wants to be everything you need and more.

I remember seeing my beautiful wife for the first time. I was in the lunchroom speaking to some friends when she walked in - I literally said to myself, she is one of the most beautiful girls I have ever seen. You better believe I did everything I could to get her attention. She was what I desired. One day she was eating M&Ms by my classroom at her locker, and I walked up to her, smiled, and asked if I could have some of the M&Ms. She smiled back and gave me some.

After some time, I realized that the feeling was mutual. What occurred first was seeing my wife, knowing that she was someone I desired, someone I wanted to love. That is when I pursued her, and that is what God did when He saw us. He said I desire to have them, and I desire to love them and be what they need and want. That is when God pursued us, thinking of amazing ways to get our attention so we can know He desires us and loves us. God does this when we do not know Him; when we are not thinking of Him, when we are not searching for Him, He finds us.

I remember seeing the movie "The Notebook" based on the 1996 romantic novel "The Notebook" written by Nicholas Sparks. In this movie, an older man is trying to get the attention of the older woman. He tries everything to get her to notice him, but nothing worked. Finally, she agrees to hear a story from him. As she is listening to the story, she becomes so interested that she asks him to read more. Now the story he reads to her was about two people who were in love. There was drama, heartbreak, and struggles in this story. The audience does not know that the older man and the woman he is reading to are the couples in the story. We realize as the movie continues that they are married, and she has Alzheimer's disease and does not recognize him.

What stands out to me is she forgot him, does not know who he is, and pays no attention to him, but because he loves her, he pursues her. He continues to show kindness and patience. At the end of the movie, he reads the last page and closes the book; she finally realizes the story is about them, and she finally displays her love for him with a hug and a kiss.

So, you see, his love for her was so powerful that it broke the chains of disease, separation, brokenness, and loneliness. In this movie, with the help of the Holy Spirit revealing more of God, the Father's heart, and His love for us. His overwhelming, never-ending, reckless love, like Bethel music, would sing. I realize when we forget about God because of distractions or circumstances that block us from communion with Him, He still pursues us with His love. He Reads us a love story about our love for each other until we remember him and expresses our love for Him in worship through singing, dancing, or words of affirmation. God loves you and will not let any stronghold, distraction, or circumstance separate you from his love. He will always come to your rescue.

Write down three things that describe how you feel, knowing how much God loves you?

This chapter talks about spending intimate time with God. Is developing intimacy with God difficult for you? What are some steps you can take to "keep the fire burning" in your relationship with the Father?

NOTES

My Glasses Are Off

3

As seen in the last chapter, knowing how much God loves you draws you closer to him. Knowing God loves you helps you to love yourself. How can there be love without God when He is love, and how can we love others when we do not love ourselves. Wow - loving yourself! I will be honest with you; that is something I struggled with for years.

When I was first born, the doctor needed to hurry the delivery process because of major swelling. While doing so, my collarbone was broken in the process. The doctor saved my life, but I was broken in the process. Because my collarbone was broken, my parents handled me with care. My mother loved me a lot more than usual. They had to be thinking, we do not want him to experience that pain again, so we will shelter him; love him. Hug and kiss him. Now I was with my mother more than my father, which led me to be like her. I was always underneath her; wherever she went, I went. I learned about affection because of her. Everyone said I was always a happy kid and that I smiled a lot.

Sidebar guys. Isn't it amazing that I experienced pain and hurt at the beginning? But because of the love and affection of my parents, I not only forgot about the earlier pain in my life, but I displayed what was shown to me. When people saw me, they could only see smiles and happiness. Look what love does. The more you experience love, the more it will take away the pain, worry, sadness and fear. You would think because of what happened at the beginning of my life that I would never want to smile. Or that I would not be a happy child. But when love is present, it changes everything.

24

Now back to the story, because I was around my mother often, I began to be a little more feminine. I started to do things with my hands that were similar gestures as a girl. Now I did not know what was going on. I spent a lot of time with my mom; I accidentally began to act like her. Now I was also shy, soft-spoken, and spoke proper English. In my neighborhood, the language was slang, so you were made fun of if you did not speak slang. My mother was not from that type of neighborhood, but my father was. Growing up in those neighborhoods was hard for me. I was made fun of, bullied on, and before my "Geauga Lake tan" (Shout out to Geauga Lake amusement park in Ohio) in high school, I was exceptionally light skin, so I was called "white mike." Even inappropriate names white people were being called, such as "white honkey" and "cracker." I experienced all of this in 2nd and 3rd grade. I was used to affection, love, and validation from my mother, but now I was around people that did not look at me like my mom did. They did not treat me as my mother did. So, I would cry all the time. I was sensitive; let me say this, being sensitive is not something as adults we should run away from. It is the sensitivity that helps you hear God more clearly. Sensitivity creates a space where no anger, hate, or pride can cause distortion. It is not like God will not speak to you; it is just that those things will try to block you from hearing God. The more sensitive you are, the more you will experience the flow of God. You will be able to push your agenda to the side and follow the plan of God.

Most would call me a cry baby. I remember one of my teachers in 3rd grade yelled at me, thinking that I needed aggression like some of the other kids: but of course, I immediately began to cry. You all should have seen her face. She was so sad that she did that. She had to comfort me. She then had the sweetest voice. See, aggression scared me, and loud noises bothered me. Therefore, I did not need to be yelled at to get my attention. I just needed someone to let me know what I should do calmly. I was not hard of hearing.

A lot happened when I was in 3rd grade; I learned that the attention of my peers was important to me. I wanted others to like me. At this time, my father began to teach me sports to toughen me up. So, I found myself loving baseball. I did not know why, but baseball was everything to me. I had baseball wallpapers all over my room. Baseball was my way out. That was something my father and I could connect with. At one point, I wasn't too close with my dad, but you should have seen the smile on his face when I began to advance in baseball. In sports, I found a connection with my father. So, I practiced, and I practiced, to make him proud. And not just in baseball, but in basketball and football as well.

In 3rd grade, it was a lot of pressure on me. I was dealing with people at school and people in my neighborhood and family. I was innocent, gullible, and I trusted everyone. There was someone in my life that saw that side of me and began to use it to their advantage. They would hug me in inappropriate ways, kiss me, and bite me. At this age, I did not know what was going on. I could not understand what was going on. Thank God for my parents praying for me because this person did not go below the belt with any inappropriate touching. But what they were doing was inappropriate. I tried to ignore it.

I always saw my parents together, so I knew one day I would be married, but at that time, I was not thinking about girls; I was focused on school and just being a kid. From 3rd grade – 6th grade, I experienced being bullied and talked about, not to mention being touched by a person older than me. It was a lot for a 7 or 8-year-old to deal with.

Please know that I am sharing this to help you realize that we do not know all our children's experiences. What we can do for them is be an ear and listen to understand them. Let them express themselves. If you see them act out for attention, watch them closely, and understand they are not experts in verbally expressing themselves. Let us create honest communication with them where they are not afraid of us. You cannot say, my kids can speak to me anytime, but you always create an environment of fear where they think twice before choosing to keep it to themselves. You will not always be around your children, so create that atmosphere where they can tell you anything that will help them and you.

Now in 6th-grade, things started to change, and I was interested in girls' attention. I remember a girl I was interested in asked if I had ever kissed a girl before; I lied and said yes. Then she said, "We will see after lunch." I said to myself, oohhhh no, I am not ready. I went to the restroom, trying to practice on my hand. Ha-ha, I was trying to remember what I watched on those old movies my father would watch. Just know that after lunch, I heard the girl I was interested in was not going to be the one that kisses me. It was going to be the most experienced girl in the class that I was not interested in. So that ended the special intimate first kiss experience that I'd seen in the movies. After this experience, I felt different; I looked at everything differently. And now I had a new focus - more attention from girls. That is when I started to distance myself from my mother. I began to slack on my schoolwork. I thought now was the time to have a girlfriend, but none of the girls wanted me. They would say to me: "I look at you as a friend or a brother." I was tired of it because they would not say that to my older brother, Willie. They would become his girlfriend. Nobody knew my name: I was called little Willie. for two years, I experience girls deny me and talk about me. Seventh grade was the last straw; there was an incident between my brother and I that left me crying in front of everyone. I then said that I would never cry again. I immediately began to harden my heart and say that I did not care about anything anymore.

I started to pay attention to my voice; seeing that it was so high, I tried to do all I could to make my voice lower. I used to sing full soprano growing up. I stopped that and moved myself to the tenor section purposely. I began to learn slang and practice it until it sounded just like the guys in the neighborhood. I put a hold on schoolwork and sports to watch movies of ladies' men or movies and shows that had a nerd turning into a smooth guy. I watched and studied this until it became me. Then I realized the only thing left to change was my appearance.

I did not like my eyes, so I thought that if I wore glasses, they would cover my imperfections. I knew my mother would not give me glasses for no reason, so I started to read in the dark. I remember her telling me often if "you read in the dark, you will hurt your eyes." She knew I loved to read; I completed many reading programs while growing up. I received free pizza and free tickets to baseball games as rewards. Reading and writing became a passion of mines that led to me writing a book about baseball released in the Young Authors Exhibit.

Therefore, it was not weird for me to read at various times of the night, but I had a plan this time. I wanted to persuade the doctor that I needed glasses. I convinced my mom to schedule me an appointment. The doctor asked for me to read the lines with one eye. My right eye was flawless - I read every line without any problems. Then he moved to the left eye, and shockingly, I struggled with a couple of lines, but it was not severe. The doctor said, "He can purchase glasses but only use them for reading." That was music to my ears, knowing that I'd completed my goal, and now I could wear glasses to cover my flaws. I ordered a pair of glasses I felt looked good on me. The sad thing was, I had to wait two weeks for the glasses to arrive. I was so excited that I kept preparing the new me by watching movies and practicing my smooth-talking abilities.

When I finally received my glasses, I also bought a new outfit. It was time to change my whole look. It was 8th grade by now, and I went to school wearing the glasses for the first time. Immediately my confidence was higher. I started to flirt and use some of the swag and demeanor that I saw in the movies. On that day, I began to get the response I was looking for from the girls I was approaching. My friend Myles Smith saw how the girls were looking at me and said to me: "It must be the glasses," and after that day, I said, "I can never take these glasses off."

I wanted attention; I wanted to be noticed. My older brothers were all popular, and I was not. Nevertheless, that all changed for me; I started to be respected in my neighborhood. The people that used to talk about me began to ask me for advice. I watched so many movies about love, romance, and relationships that I thought I was an expert. I started calling myself "The Love Doctor." That name followed me wherever I went. I always wanted to be a counselor, so I felt it was a step in the right direction. People would call me and ask for advice regarding their relationships, and most of the time, I gave good advice. I became popular in school.

Two things I was known for in high school were always carrying gum and giving relationship advice! I was a hopeless romantic, so I loved to help relationships work. I helped a lot of people, but I could never help myself. When I first approached a girl, I would use all my movie knowledge to make them laugh or charm them. As soon as they were my girlfriend, I did not know what to do. The real me would come out. The clingy, always wanting to be in their face, longing for long phone conversations, wanting to give and receive affection version of myself became too much for some of them. I have heard on countless occasions that I was too good for a person. Who breaks up with people because they are too good to them? Therefore, I changed! I realized I did not want commitment. I would rather have fun and stay away from titles. And that is when I began to hurt people and shut people out. I never tried to do it on purpose. I was just tired of being hurt, so I put up a wall. I would advise people to talk about their problems and work out their issues with their partners, but I would run from my problems and avoid conflict as much as possible. I lost who I was. I battled being myself compared to what everyone else wanted me to be. I remember a girl saying that I was conceited, and I thought to myself, "you don't have a clue," but then she said, I'm not talking about you and your looks. I am talking about when you open your mouth and speak. And she was right; when I opened my mouth, I would say the boldest and most confident things to a girl that I would

30

not have said if a mirror was present. When you are in front of people you can only see them, so you forget what you look like and speak. You can imagine that you are the best-looking person in the world even when you do not believe it. I could never keep up with it because the real me would eventually show up. Every time I revealed the real me, I hated it. I started to hate myself. I was broken and did not know how to express myself. How could I be me when no one likes the real me?

I was very observant and loved knowledge; that is why I clung to the older crowd. I remember people would call me Grandpa because my thought processes were like those of an older generation. So, I kept wearing the glasses. I needed them. My identity was in the glasses. The weird thing is, in the movies, people took off their glasses to be cool, but I put them on to be cool. I did not realize the battle with loving myself. It had nothing to do with the glasses. The glasses were my mask.

I had no identity. I then saw that most people's actions come from a root. Most of the time, we look at the negative, weird actions, and we never ask or dig deeper to find where those actions came from. When we see a bad attitude, someone angry, a very flirtatious person, or someone who lies a lot, try to ask what happened for them to end up like this? This perspective will get rid of several misunderstandings, arguments, fights, and judgments. All of us have a story, and some are embarrassed to share their story. Some are ashamed and even scared. Those people who feel ashamed to share their stories are just looking for someone who will say to them, "I am not afraid of your story because this is not the end." Better days are coming. I thank God for my wife; she wasn't afraid to dig deep and find the cause of the

31

problem, and when she did, she wasn't afraid to share them. "One day, I can write another book about that story, but for now, I will fast forward to the day I got rid of the glasses. Remember, the doctor said to wear them for reading purposes only, but that turned into wearing them every second of the day for eight years. For eight years, I wore glasses, never needing them, but I could never take them off. My wife is the first person that insisted I take them off when she saw me. Even when we were dating, she would always compliment me or say, "Hey, I like you without the glasses." I always thought she was crazy! But she was planting a seed. I know you all are wondering, when did I officially take the glasses off? Well, I will let you guess

Did I take them off on my wedding day?
Or
When my singing group, Nu Covenant, appeared on America's Got Talent?

It was not when I got married to my wife. I told her I was not going to ruin our wedding pictures by not wearing glasses. Insecurity had a hold on me. I was in a cage. It was like the quote from the movie Lucy, "It's hard to focus on anything else when all you can see is pain." Many in this world struggle with loving themselves because all they can see is hurt, insecurity, guilt, shame, unforgiveness, feeling inadequate, and not feeling qualified, feeling misunderstood, and even bullied. A lot of people wear a mask because they are afraid people will not like the real them. So, they act until they forget who they are. That was me until God came to my rescue. God knows that He has everything I need to feel complete, to feel validated. God wants you to know who you are and how He sees you. God is perfect, and in His

32

presence, there is perfection; there is freedom from insecurity, fear, depression, and anxiety. That is why it is important to know how much God loves you. To know He cares and wants the best for you. Knowing this will help you to see yourself the way God sees you. Beautiful, powerful, unique, forgiven, qualified, holy, blameless, and righteous. If you struggle to see yourself like this, it is a sign that you need more time in God's presence.

My group, Nu Covenant, had the opportunity to appear on the show America's Got Talent (thanks to my wife again for signing us up). When we heard that we would appear on the show, our manager at the time, Charlea Watkins, knew a stylist's name, Charles Sheppard, who looked at all of us and gave advice on what we needed to change or keep. He looked at me and said, everything is good, except you need to get rid of those glasses and wear contacts. My heart dropped; I could not believe the day finally came where I needed to get rid of my crutch, my mask, what I put my identity in. I asked the stylist, with tears in my eyes, for him to come into the other room so we could talk. I had to tell him he was asking for an impossible task. He saw tears in my eyes and asked, "Michael, for real, what is the real issue?" I then told him everything. Thank God he did not budge, he encouraged me and said I could reach out to him if it gets hard, but he told me to get rid of the glasses for the group's sake. So, I did. I went home to my wife and told her everything with tears running down my face. She smiled at me, gave me some advice, and let me know she was with me. You know she could have said, "What is wrong with you? Don't you know my opinion is all that matters?" But no, she was there for me the whole way. I later made my first appearance on America's Got Talent without glasses, and I never put them back on again. Our group would later make it to the top 48 contestants of the show before being eliminated. God wanted me to let go of the glasses because it was a blinder. How could I truly know who I am when I was always hiding behind a mask? I had to learn how to love myself, and God is the one who was there to show me.

NOTES

My Transformation

4

Without the glasses, I was vulnerable; I lacked confidence. I knew something was missing, so I began to push in for a spiritual awakening. I was hungry for more. I remember my parents were in college at the time. I'm so proud of them as they graduated with their bachelor's degree in their 50s. As they were in college for Religious Studies and Christian Counselling, they began to learn things they did not know before. They realized some of the things spoken to them were untrue. They saw that our culture taught us things and revealed the problems that arose because of it. We started to have home Bible studies about the new things my parents learned. It was fun and exciting.

At one point in time, 19 people were living in my parents' house. My parents are the kindest people ever. They allowed families to live in their homes along with several individuals and young men in particular. My parents did this for years. I grew up seeing many people living in the house until they found a place of their own. I love my parents for that. Even when my wife and I moved out of my parents' house, they still loved us and made sure we had everything we needed. They not only cared about us spiritually, but they cared about our natural needs too. My parents going to college helped open my mind to more possibilities.

I also think that going to college helped as well. My critical thinking class enabled me to see the importance of looking from someone else's perspective. To know that everyone has a different opinion and that is okay. We all do not think alike; our environments teach us and can influence our reality. I graduated with an associate degree in business. I was a full-time musician at that time, but I learned a lot that I continue to use today. All these experiences forced me to question my spirituality and what I believed. Some people are afraid to question their spirituality, but this is good. How can you know what you believe if you do not question it?

I knew something was missing. I knew that I was stuck. Remember, earlier in the book, I said that I believed God was mean. God being love was barely spoken about in my community. It was more about "do not do this and do not do that." The message was always, if you do not want to be punished, then act perfect. I am not going to lie; it was starting to sound impossible to me. I would hear people say you need to ask for forgiveness every second of the day, or before you ask God for anything, make sure you say a certain phrase first. I heard people say He is a forgiving God, but only after asking Him to forgive you. So, if you do not ask for forgiveness, then you are not forgiven. People would speak about eternal damnation every Sunday and only speak about heaven at a funeral. I was stuck and tired. I needed freedom, so I started to ask God to reveal Himself to me. I wanted Him to show me who He is.

Who are you?
Are you there?
Do you exist?
And if you do exist, do you love us?

I started to go to every worship service held. My mom would even have a prayer service in her bedroom. It was a 3-night prayer service in her bedroom! See, that's real fellowship, real church. I remember something different happened to me that day, almost like the disciples in one room waiting for the gift of the Holy Spirit. I was waiting for a real encounter with God, waiting for a shift, for something to happen. Something did happen; I had this overwhelming feeling come over me that I knew was different. I do not remember all of it because I woke up on the bare floor, and I know no one pushed me. I came out of the bedroom - revival pumped. I just knew I received that gift that Jesus promised.

The Holy Spirit. I rejoiced, but days later, I started to doubt. I did not know that the Holy Spirit was a gift that God wanted to give to us. We do not have to beg, and then he decides if we are worthy to receive it. The gift equips you to be a better person. This gift helps you to be like God. Why would God withhold that from you? He wants the best for you, and he knows holding wisdom, revelations, and a spirit that will bring you into all truth is not beneficial to you. Giving you the gift is beneficial. If anyone reading this book thinks that God has forgotten about you, know he has not. The scriptures say in Luke 11:11-13 NLT, "You fathers if your children ask for a fish, do you give them a snake instead? Or if they ask for an egg, do you give them a scorpion? Of course not!" It later goes on to say if we know how to give good gifts to our children, how much more will your heavenly Father give the Holy Spirit to those who ask him. If you ask, you will receive.

I know some of you are wondering, "how will you know that you have received the Holy Spirit"? That is where faith comes in. Faith is why we believe in a God we can't see but can feel and hear. In some denominations, they believe the evidence of receiving the Holy Spirit is speaking in tongues and remember its evidence meaning to prove something or to make plain or clear. Therefore, yes, speaking in tongues is evidence and proof that you have received the Holy Spirit, but that does not mean that's the only way to prove you have received the gift. Remember receiving is a faith thing - you receive what you believe. So, if you ask for the Holy Spirit, and you receive. Just know, if you do not believe in tongues, then you will not speak. It is also a gift, and if you do not want the gift or are afraid of the gift like I once was, it will not manifest. To be clear, the Holy Spirit is the gift that keeps on giving; it's like a preacher I heard, David Schafer, said, "A watermelon contains 200 seeds, and each seed produces a vine, and each vine produces. The seeds of just one watermelon can produce 400 more watermelons." Now, you can feed more than yourself. And that is the Holy Spirit; when you have the Holy Spirit, this spirit brings gifts – these gifts help you relate well with life issues and impact more lives.

Therefore, when a person receives the Holy Spirit, they receive all the gifts of the Spirit, but they choose which one to operate in based on their measure of faith. The gifts of the Holy Spirit as explained by the book of 1 Corinthians 12 are the word of wisdom, word of knowledge, faith, the gift of healing, the gift of working of miracles, the gift of prophecy, gift of discernment of spirits, and the gift of interpretation of tongues. We all can operate in all the gifts, but not all of us believe that we can, so we remain satisfied that we have the Spirit inside us. I remember telling myself, "When you receive the Holy Spirit, you're not going to speak in tongues because that is weird or crazy looking." For those who do not know anything about speaking in tongues, speaking, or praying in tongues is a revelation gift. It is a gift that breaks down the mysteries of God's word and character in a way you can personally understand. Thank God for one of my mentors,

42

Michael Kelley, and his mentor Dave Roberson, who wrote the book "The Walk of the Spirit, the Walk of Power." They are the reason I know about tongues and the importance of that gift.

Love Without Strings

5

Most people are afraid of the unknown, but we all are attracted to the supernatural; that's why some enjoy superheroes, magic, miracles, angels, astrology, technology, and even fortune cookies. Who does not like a good fortune cookie? We are so attracted to the supernatural because we are created by a Supernatural being whose presence is felt everywhere. That is why some people love to be surrounded by nature, because of the beauty, the sense of belonging. The peace it presents. I remember my parents having a house on the east side of Cleveland - this house had a section where you could climb out of the house and sit on the roof. Every night I would go on the top and think, relax, and admire the view. I was able to see downtown Cleveland and witness the stars. The fullness of nature did not surround me, and I was still able to tap into the amazing atmosphere, the incredible presence of our Creator.

With a couple of spiritual practices, I was able to understand more about my personality. I was able to see that God genuinely loved me. I was asked a question one day, "If I told my daughter not to play in the street and she disobeyed and did it anyway, would I throw my daughter in front of a car to punish her for not listening to me?" I said no. The person later said, so why would God put sickness on you to punish you for your mistakes.

At that time, I could not process all of it. I would sit at home in my room asking God, "Are you a punisher? Are you mad at me?" I would pace the floor, asking these questions over and over until God revealed the mysteries of His love to me. I learned that God thought about me often. I would turn YouTube on and play songs that explained God's love for me. Tears would come to my eyes when I realized I did not have to do anything to make him love me. Most would say people only love you for what you can do for them, but you do not have to worry about that with God. His love for you is not based on what you can do for Him. When my daughter Isabella was about 1-year-old, I had a revelation about God's love for us. I looked at her and smiled, saying to myself, wow, why do I love you so much. Knowing she could not do anything for me. I fed her, provided for her, protected her, and she could not say thank you or say she loves me. I will ask you the same thing God asked me, "What can she do to make you love her more than you already do right now?" My answer was nothing. There is nothing she can do to make me love her more than I did at that moment.

And that is when a light bulb went off in my head. I realized there is nothing I can do to make God love me more than He does right now. He loves me, protects me, and provides for me because I am His child. Tears came to my eyes. I learned it is good to let the tears flow when you feel them coming. That is the purging process, the time where transformation is happening. It is a time where the things that are hurting you or bothering you fall off. Next, is God filling you up with His love. His comforting presence comes and visits you and builds you up. His presence comes and ministers to you that you are loved. He creates an atmosphere where you feel that you can be honest and willing to open your heart to Him and allow Him to speak affirmations to your spirit. People can be vulnerable and honest when there is an atmosphere of peace, mercy, and a judge-free zone.

Have you ever thought of one reason why most people lie? It is because they are afraid of the outcome, fearful of punishment, afraid to disappoint someone. I encourage all of you to create a space of peace, mercy, and a judge-free zone, and you will see more truth. People will not be afraid to put themselves in the light. They will desire to be in the light because light ends darkness, like the group L.E.D would say. There is freedom in the light; we only hide what we think is embarrassing or what may result in punishment. But what if no punishments were coming? What if there was an embrace coming for the embarrassing secret we held? We would reveal our secret if we knew there was mercy and love present. We will finally experience freedom from the toxic buildup of holding hurtful information, from keeping embarrassing secrets that you knew could affect someone. That is how I felt in God's presence. I felt that I could finally be honest. I finally met someone that was not afraid of my story. I finally met someone that would not say, "You can tell me the secret, I won't be mad," and then make you regret telling them. God is not like that. He knows everything I do, and He still finds ways to make me happy. God still finds ways to provide for me knowing I make mistakes. He still finds ways to show me He loves me.

In my wife's and I first, place together the furnace went out. We knew the owner would have to fix it if it was broken, so we started to use the oven to heat the house, but then the oven broke. We had a heater, and we used it to warm up the bedroom. At this time, we only had one daughter, Angelina, who would sleep in the crib right next to us. It was so cold in the other rooms that we would have to put coats on to walk to the bathroom. No lie, guys, it was real. And our car had broken down on our street. Thank God for my parents, who would pick us up for service or pick us up to go to the grocery store. All of this was going on and one of my mentors, Michael Kelley, whom I had just met,

47

picked me up to see what things he and his family would need to sing at our event. Now while I was with him, he said to me, "Michael, you know God loves you, and He wants you to have a working car." He also told me to wake up every morning, look out the window, and say, "Father, I thank you that I have a working car." I did not know what would happen after I said these words, but I knew I had nothing else to lose. I was at my lowest point.

So, I did what he said; I woke up every morning saying just that. We had a mechanic coming to the house telling us what could be wrong with the car, but nothing was working. Until one day, we received a call, and the mechanic said the car is working! I was amazed and began to rejoice. He said there was a security lock on it. The vehicle would lock down sometimes if it felt a theft alert. The car sat in front of the house for three months until I started speaking and thanking God for a working vehicle. Somehow one of the workers had a thought to try the manual security unlock code. We now know angels spoke to that young man and told him exactly what needed to be completed. You already know after this experience, I was pumped. I knew it was time to push a little deeper.

So, I did; I became a sponge soaking in the knowledge needed to grow spiritually. Like I said earlier in the book, you cannot know someone unless you spent time with them. So, I scheduled personal time in God's presence. Every night I would sit in a quiet room and receive from God, allowing His Spirit to teach me the things of God, His heart, and character. I was hungry for knowledge. A preacher said one time the Lord prepared a table before us, but it is our choice to eat. I prayed all the time; I allowed that heavenly language to flow through me every chance I got. At that time, I did not know if what I was doing was working. I just kept praying. I would hear from my mentors no matter what happens; keep praying. So, I did. That is when I noticed something different. I started to wake up, receiving revelations and answers to questions I was asking. My wife and I use to babysit our friend's son, Marcus. Every morning at 4 am she would drop him off. I could not go back to sleep. My thoughts would keep running, preventing me from sleeping. I did not know what was going on then, but later I realized that God was speaking to me, answering my questions, revealing the truth of what I was pondering on. It was amazing; it was like a boost, like hundreds of light bulbs turning on.

This experience was huge for me because I told a few of my mentors' months before that I could not hear from God. I was trying to figure out, did He speak audibly? To this day, I have not heard His voice audibly. I have only experienced a thought come across my mind, and I realize I am not smart enough to think about that particular thought. Have you ever experienced a thought that directed you to go a certain way or lead you to avoid a certain path? Later you realized the thought/voice was correct. Know that place is where you hear His voice. God is a spirit, and we have a spirit so we can communicate with Him. Sometimes, when He speaks, you will think it is your thoughts or you speaking to yourself, but it is Him speaking to you. I call it "paying attention to your thoughts." You will know it is God by the good thoughts. The thoughts of love, peace, kindness, and goodness. Any thought to harm you or someone else is not God. God is not in bullying, cyberbullying, judging others, or using words to tear down. He is about building up, comforting, healing, and restoring. I did not believe this earlier in my spiritual walk, but when I had my encounter in His presence, that all changed. See, I used to be a believer in punishment and God being mad at you. If someone were mad at you, wouldn't the time come if you were in their presence for them to show you how angry they are at you? Well, that is not what happened to me. I entered God's presence, and where I should have felt pain, I felt love, and where I should have felt anger, I felt peace. Where I should have experienced sickness, I experienced healing. That is like someone telling you, "When you finally see this person, he or she is going to hurt you, show you how angry he or she is. There will be no mercy." If someone told you this, how shocked would you be to be in their presence, and they hug you instead of hitting you. Speak peace into your life. Love you instead of hurting you. Your whole perspective will change, also the way you see that person. So, although people were saying this is what the person is like or this is how they feel, you realize it is best to find out from the source. Find out who the person is and not what you heard. The spirit of God brings love, peace, faithfulness, joy, goodness, gentleness, patience, self-control, and kindness. If God is all those things, it made sense why I felt this way. Being in the presence of God will always result in those wonderful, uplifting experiences.

Jesus displayed compassion, healing, restoration, and, most importantly, forgiveness. Look at Mark 2:1-12. There was a paralyzed man, and four men arrived at the house where Jesus was. They could not get in the house because it was full. That did not stop the men. They dug a hole through the roof and lowered the man right in front of Jesus. Jesus saw the four men, looked at the paralyzed man, and said, your sins are forgiven. What stuck out to me is that Jesus forgives the man's sin without the man asking for forgiveness. WOW!! He never asked Jesus to forgive his sins. This revelation ended me asking for

50

forgiveness every second of the day. Ephesians 2:8 NIV says, "For it is by grace you have been saved through faith, and this is not from yourselves (meaning you can't take credit for this). It is a gift from God." Wow, here we go again, more gifts from God. Let's pay attention to this scripture, for it is by grace (invisible power that transforms) you have been saved (healed, set free, made whole); you can't take credit for this (a source of pride or honor). Credit (time allowed for payment) is a gift (something given with no strings attached). All of this is access through faith. Faith will access everything, including forgiveness. Faith will create an atmosphere of heaven, even the benefits of heaven such as healing, prosperity, grace, forgiveness, and so much more than we can imagine. It is the key to unlocking everything we need and desire.

I started to realize that God knows my heart. He is not insecure or needs validation where He needs an apology to feel happy or a reason to bless me or take care of my needs. He is not sitting on the throne saying, "I'm not helping Michael reach his destiny" or "I'm not helping him financially or spiritually until he apologizes." That is what I used to believe, and that is something that we experience in our culture and society. Society says you cannot experience sympathy, restoration, or forgiveness until you apologize. Sometimes we forget about the people that have forgiven others without receiving an apology.

I have experienced times where I was mistreated by people and never received an apology. At the time, I was upset and did not want to be around them, but I entered the presence of God, and it was like all pain and anger left. To this day, those people never apologized, and I treat them like it never happened. If I am capable of forgiving others with no apology, a perfect God must be able to do the same thing. It would not make sense that a human could do this but not God. You will have to say then that I am more forgiving than God. And we all know that is not possible.

Let us look at another story of Jesus. Before he was crucified, he told his disciples that one would betray Him, one will deny Him and the others will scatter, basically leaving Him. Jesus knew that all of this would happen, and He still decided to save them. How many people, knowing that everyone was going to leave at the most critical time in their lives, would continue to love them. How many would still die for people like that? That is why one of my favorite scriptures is Romans 5:8 NLT: "God showed his great love for us by sending Christ to die for us while we were still sinners." In this scripture, it does not say He died for us when we got ourselves together. It did not say when we fixed ourselves that's when God showed His great love. This scripture says while we didn't know His name, while we were doing whatever we wanted, while we knew He existed but denied ever knowing Him, that's when He showed His great love for us. Why? Because God knew if Jesus is lifted up, he will draw all men to Him. Wow! God loves us. He wants to love. He desires to show love. He finds fulfillment in doing so. That is why one of the apostles from the Bible, Paul, said, "I am persuaded that nothing can separate me from the love of God" (Romans 8:38 KJV). Why? Because love is everywhere because God is everywhere.

Michael asked these questions of God:

Who are you?

Are you there?

Do you exist?

And if you do exist, do you love us?

Do you find yourself asking similar questions of God?

Michael shared how his childhood experiences shaped his battle with self-love and insecurities. How have your childhood experiences shaped your battles with self-love and insecurities?

List 3 events you believe have affected this area of your life. How have they shown up in how you interact with others and think about yourself? How have they impacted your relationship with God?

Have you ever struggled with working for God's love?

NOTES

Revelation of Grace and Mercy

6

My life was transformed; I saw God in a new way. A loving Father that is not ashamed of his son. A Father that draws people in with love and provides everything we need and desire. I started to share this information with everyone, especially my family. I did not know everything, and I still do not, but what I found out through praying, worshipping, and personal intimacy with God, I cannot undo what I learned and experienced. The knowledge of His love was alive to me. This knowledge was freedom. Those experiences in His presence saved my life. I knew my purpose, my destiny, and that was to help people come into the knowledge of God's love for them. I saw my life change. I stopped focusing on my insecurities, flaws, shortcomings, and sins. Focusing on those things made me worse. The more I wanted to stop being insecure, the more I became insecure. When I focused on not sinning or being angry, I found sin, and my anger increased. But a light shined on me, a light so bright that I could not focus on anything else but God's love for me. I realized I had no power; I could not fix myself. I realized God has the power to transform my life, so I allowed His grace to come.

Thank God for my god brother, Quentin Johnson, for helping me to see the difference in grace and mercy. Here is what he told me, "Mercy is God's compassion on humanity. God's compassion that understands empathizes, and sympathizes with human emotions, thoughts, and actions." We may have thought mercy is when someone deserves punishment but receives a 2nd chance. But no, that's not mercy; that's "Human toleration." Have you ever heard the phrase, "You are getting on my nerves,"; "You are walking on thin ice with me,"; "This is the last straw," or "I love you, but I don't have to like you." Imagine the times someone said or thought that phrase and kept it hidden and just decided to tolerate the person. Wanting to retaliate and cause some harm, but saying to themselves, no, I will ignore it this time and give them another chance to fix the situation.

So, what is mercy since we know what Mercy is NOT? Mercy is compassion, showing sympathy for one another. Mercy is empathy, identifying yourself as they are. Mercy is love; when you embrace someone in their pain, you contribute to easing their pain or making it easy for them to bear. Yes! Mercy is all these things.

Grace is the divine inspiration of God upon your heart with its outward reflection upon your life. Basically, the powers that work in us. Grace changes you from the inside, by the Holy Spirit. to reveal what God looks like on the outside. Thank God for Quentin because I used to combine the words mercy and grace, thinking they were the same. I used to hear that "Grace is unmerited favor," but when they would explain what unmerited favor is, they would say, "It's God's way of showing mercy," never separating the two, keeping both meanings the same. But they are not the same. Grace is the reason we see a transformation in our lives. It is an invisible power that comes to heal, restore, and complete. Here is an example of God's grace that came to me in my time of pondering about grace.

My younger brother, Marc McMillon, broke his femur bone at the age of five. He had to wear a half-body cast. Please pay attention to the process happening while he wore the cast because, without the cast, it was impossible to help the healing process. Marc later would be fit for sports again. He was one of the fastest people playing. So, the question is, what healed him? What happened while he wore the cast?

The doctors knew that there was an invisible power that would heal him from the inside out. The doctors created an opportunity for the body to heal itself. And now, when everyone sees my brother, they do not see the broken Marc; they see the 100% Marc. There was an invisible power that healed, restored, and completed the process. That is why I stopped focusing on my broken pieces because I cannot fix them. I need the grace of God to come and do its work where I can experience transformation, where I can experience wholeness. If I know there is grace for me, then guess what, there is grace for us all!

Keeping in mind the definitions given for Mercy and Grace, how have these gifts worked in your life? List examples.

NOTES

Loving People

7

When we experience the love and kindness of God, it draws us closer
to God and then motivates us to love people.

#lovedraws (Nu Covenant)

Loving people comes from the revelation that God loves you,
and you are no different from everyone else in the world. If you know
that God wants the best for you, then He also wants the best for others.
Sometimes we struggle with stinginess because society has taught us
there is not enough. That there is lack and limitations. That is not true,
God; our Father owns everything, so that means prosperity is ours, all
our needs are met, and even our desires. So, when we take on that
perspective, we begin to give and help our brothers and sisters. As I
started to grow in the knowledge of God's love for me, I began to share
that knowledge with everyone, starting with my family.

I would share my revelations with my wife, brothers, sister,
friends, and parents. I was excited because I realized this amazing God
wanted the best for us. Imagine the wealthiest and most powerful
human in the world calls you on your phone and says, "Whatever you
need and desire, I will get for you, don't be afraid to ask me." Then
they say, "Matter of fact, whoever asks me, I will do the same for
them." If you heard this, would you be excited? Yes! You will tell
everyone you know that someone is willing to take care of all their
needs. I went around spreading the good news of our Father's love for
us all. I encouraged everyone to start spiritual practices to help with the
transformation of their souls (mind, emotions, and intellect). I
also encouraged them to focus on hearing God's voice clearly and
seeing people the way God sees them. We all are children of God,
which comes with benefits such as protection, healing, salvation,

prosperity, peace, love, and joy. All of this is activated by faith, believing in God, the one who is all those things. I traveled around encouraging others to believe in God, a Father that will not leave you, a Father that will not abandon you. A Father that will not run away when times are hard. A Father of love that is patient and kind. A humble Father, a Father that wants to listen to you, a Father that loves to hear your voice, to listen to your song. A Father who loves to read your story. A Father who loves to listen to your ideas and loves to help those ideas come into existence. A Father that smiles on your heart because He knows whatever He creates is beautiful and good. Come on! Just reading this helps place a fire in our hearts that depression cannot put out, that anxiety cannot put out. When you see people the way God sees them, like a beautiful person that has a purpose and destiny, a person that God loves just as much as He loves you, you begin to be God's hands, His feet, His voice. You begin to be the proof of His love like the singing group.

"For King & Country" sings.
"Let my life be the proof of his love."
"Let my love look like you and what it's made of."
"How you live, how you died."
"Love is sacrifice."

The revelation of loving people helped my wife and I go around to different restaurants paying for family meals without telling them. My singing group Nu Covenant calls it "Stringless Love" - giving without strings being attached. My favorite place to go on Sundays was Steak & Shake; we would go every Sunday after service. We did not have a lot of money, but we saw a revelation and could not shake it. At this restaurant, you paid the bill at the counter. So, I would pay for my family's meal and then asked the clerk for the bill for a particular table. Most of the time, we picked tables with families because we knew the sacrifice of taking kids out to eat. I would pay and write God loves you on their receipt. To this day, they will never know who paid for their meal unless they are reading this book!

We realize that God owns everything, so there is nothing we can give Him that He does not already have. Therefore, the question is, how can we thank Him for the things He has given or the amazing things He has done for us? We can thank Him by giving to others. In I John 4, it says if a person says they love God whom they cannot see but hate their brothers and sisters who they can see, they are a liar. Therefore, we cannot say "I love God" and forget everyone else. We cannot say, "It's just God and me," no. If we say we love God, it will show by the way we love people. We show God, we love Him by loving people. Giving money is one way to show love because this world uses money to take care of needs and desires. There are many more ways we can show love to one another. You can also give a hug, words of encouragement, prophetic words (speaking good in their future), or even a phone call or text is good enough to show love in this world.

I used to say, "The world would be a better place if parents never took away our pacifiers" haha (sorry, that was a dad joke). I now know that if we can operate in love, we will see less stealing and no murders because not only will we love our neighbor, but we will love the family that loves our neighbor. We all will have everything we need because of the kindness of people. We will want everyone to have what they need and enough left over to get what they desire. This perspective is the first plan of the Father, to create a place that there is no lack and no worry. The problem is that pride and greed have hit and took us off course, but God the Father is coming like He promised to restore his first plan. Many people try to make the end times scary like God is so angry He is ready to destroy everything, but He is happy to finally have his children living in a place of peace, no death, and abundance. As we wait for that beautiful day, we can live on this earth, building up our brothers & sisters.

NOTES

My Experiences with Spiritual Gifts

8

At GFT (Greater Fair Temple), a man we had never seen before asked my father if he could share a few words. I love my father because he does not mind giving someone the space to share their heart. So far, the service was awesome; people expressed their love to God by singing and dancing. We started service at 11:15 am, and when the man asked to share what was on his heart, the time was 3:30 pm. So, our record for being at service was broken. The man gets up and says, "Hey, I know it's late, but if you don't mind staying, I will give a word to everyone in here; whoever needs to leave, they can." I was shocked after hearing him say that. How can he do that? How can he hear a word from God for everyone present? This man gave a prophetic word to everyone that stayed. We did not leave service until 5 pm. It was like he knew what people were thinking. He also spoke for some future events to happen that did happen.

I know now he was operating in the gifts of prophecy and words of knowledge. I remember saying to myself, "I want to operate like that." People left church encouraged, uplifted, motivated, and I wanted to be a part of that. I love to help people, and what better way for them to know that God was thinking of them by using a stranger to share information to help with their purpose and destiny. Then I started seeking knowledge and the opportunity to prophesy and operate in the gift of words of knowledge. I would ask God daily for the chance to operate as I saw from the prophet who visited our service. I was not open to spiritual practices such as praying in tongues, worship, meditation (what I consider pondering), but the desire to operate like that prophet helped change my mind. I was open to anything. I was eager to learn and progress. This is one of the reasons why it was easier to listen to my mentors. Even if it was hard to believe, I knew there was more out there, and I wanted to learn what it was. I knew God wanted to use people to show His love, His glory, His power. I wanted to be one of His people.

I came across many people that did not believe in God. It was not because they did not have a sense of a higher power or a creator of this world. They did not believe in a mean God. A God of punishment. To tell you the truth, I do not believe in that God either. I hope that by seeing the earlier examples mentioned in this book, you will start to see God as a loving Father who wants the best for you, who has incredible patience and doesn't rejoice when you fail or fall. Let me ask you a question, what true loving fathers will wish bad upon their children when they are trying to walk? What father sees their child tripping over toys or things in their way and tells them to give up because they will never walk? What father yells at their child, trying to walk, to stop falling? What father says to the child, if you fall again, I will find the punishment that fits this situation? A loving father sees a child trying to walk, and immediately a smile appears on that father's face, and he begins to root his child on. That father begins to surround that child with open arms. Knowing the child will fall, he keeps picking them up while motivating them to keep going because the father knows the destination. The father knows they will one day walk. Ask a father how they felt when they saw their child stand up and take their first step. They are excited, happy, and proud. That moment will stay in their minds forever.

This is how God the Father sees us; when we were babies (when we first believe). He took care of everything, fed us, provided for us, protected us, prayed for us, drew us with His love and kindness, and spoke into our lives. And then we begin to grow and start to crawl, desiring to move forward. God knows that we must keep growing and moving forward because if we stay where we are as babies, we will never help anyone. Then he helps us to stand and encourages us to take a step, and as we are trying to walk, we will experience bad decisions, times of failure, and even pain, but none of this is caused by God. Walking comes with obstacles; it comes with adventure where risk and danger can be present, but God focuses on the destination; God sees you being bold, reminds you that you are more than a conqueror.

Therefore, instead of stopping you from walking, knowing that you may fall or experience pain, He roots you on. He reveals that you are almost to a place of complete awareness of your destiny and purpose where you will help someone else walk and then later run. Being a father, I was so protective of my first daughter that I did not want anything to happen to her. I remember my wife would place her fingers in my daughter's hand to help her stand up and wait for her to take a step. I would be nervous looking at them. At that moment, I ignored the fact that my daughter, at some point, needs to walk. And no matter how many times my daughter fell, I knew one day she would walk. I could not do anything with my strength to help her. That was something she had to do on her own. My daughter started walking at nine months, and now she is ten years old, helping her sisters ride their bikes.

God cares about unity, family, and relationships. Why? Because He loves us all and does not want just one to walk in abundance while the next person does not. He wants us all to experience the full manifestation of the promises for our lives.

I always wanted people to understand me. I never wanted to be misunderstood. When I noticed we all have different ways of seeing God,

I said, "God, I will be your voice. I will find out your character and display it. I will spend time with you, so I don't say something that I haven't discovered in your presence." I pursued that. That was me taking a step to walk, then later help my brothers and sisters do so as well. One day, I would find what I was looking for at one of my mentor's services. I started playing there on Sunday nights to be around their family and to learn more. They invited a young speaker from Africa named Kevin Kazemi; he was young and confident. Todd White calls it "Godfidence." (Godly Confidence) I was sitting in the corner playing for the worship part of the service, and then they turned the service over to Kevin, where he spoke a little bit and then began to call out people in the crowd and give them words that God was revealing to him. I was amazed, not just how young he was, but how he was operating; he would look in the crowd and ask if someone had a particular pain in their body. Someone in the crowd would raise their hand, saying it was them. He would walk to them and command pain to leave their body, and then he would ask if the pain was still there, and they would answer no.

Now, I did see things like this happening growing up being under the ministry with my parents. They prayed for people with cancer, HIV, Hepatitis C, and all types of sickness, and then the person would go to the doctor, and the doctor would say, "Wow, what happened, where did it go?" So, I already knew about miracles; I did not know that I would be next to experience a serious miracle. Kevin looks at the crowd and says there is someone here whose jaw keeps locking up. I think to myself, wow, that is me. See, what had happened was our friend Sidney Reed used to play around and sing, and he would use his jaw to complete a singing run. It was hard to do, but my brother Marc learned it first, and then I learned next. One time, I tried it, and my jaw was stuck, and I was

76

dealing with that problem for a long time. It would scare me to yawn because I had to bring my hand to my jaw to put it back in place. When I heard Kevin ask someone to come up if their jaw was out of place. I put down my bass guitar and went in front of him. He placed his hands on my jaw and spoke, healing over it. It happened in less than 10 seconds, then I walked away, purposely yawning, trying to see if my jaw was healed. And guess what? It was! Yes, I was shocked too.

I realized that I needed that experience because, at that period, I was tired of tradition. I was tired of doing the same thing every day, not knowing what was real and what wasn't. We live in a society that thinks having an imagination is immature. We are taught to only believe with our natural eyes. We were taught only to help people that are helping us. These teachings stay in our heads and create a perspective and reality to live by. I was tired and ready for a deeper connection. I was ready to step out of the boat and walk on water. So, after service was over, I asked him, "how did you do that? Did God tell you those things, and how did you know you were correct"?

Thank God Kevin is a cool, laid-back guy, or he likes my bass guitar playing. He sat down beside me in the first row and started answering my questions. I remember him using the word practice. He told me to practice hearing the voice. My brain immediately put up a red flag, flashbacking to some seasoned believers (that is another word for old!). I remember they would shame the word practice when it came to anything concerning God, but I kept listening to Kevin because I couldn't deny what I saw and experienced with my own eyes. So, I asked, "practice? How do you practice hearing the voice?" He gave me some great advice; he told me to "wake up and ask the holy spirit to show you who will be the first person you see today and see if you see or heard right." I know Kevin had to see my face and said, ok, let me tell you another one. He then said, "If you see someone you don't know while walking down the street, ask the Holy Spirit to give you a word for them and go to that person and see if the information you heard is right. You have nothing to lose if you don't know them." I looked at him with determination in my eyes; my godbrother Quentin was right there with me. I told myself that I would try it the next day. There was a hunger inside me. Not only was I doing my daily spiritual practices, but now I can be the voice for the invisible God. Kevin gave me the last piece that I needed to start operating in the gift of words of knowledge (when God reveals the present or the past in someone's life or situation).

I learned that God speaks to all of us and not just the Pastors, Ministers, or everyday churchgoers. He speaks to everyone; we are His children, and He wants to communicate with us. So, I knew it was important to pay attention to our thoughts. This is where you will hear His voice. I added the last piece, and that is practicing. No one learns someone's voice after hearing them call you once. It is hearing them speak to you multiple times for you to know it is them or to be able to point them out in the crowd. I realized I needed to listen more. And then get around people to see what beautiful things God is saying about them and their current or past situations.

You best believe the next day I woke up and said, Holy Spirit, show me the first person I will see today. I saw a man on a bike with a red shirt riding down the street. At that time, I lived on the main street, so you are not seeing the same person walking the sidewalks every day. I then opened my eyes, went to the living room window, and looked outside, and saw a woman walking down the street, and I said, "Dang, I tried." And when I said that the next person, I seen was the one on the bike with a red shirt! I jumped up and said, "Oooooo, it worked." I knew then that I needed to do a little more research about this gift. I imagined how many lives can change for the better because I was willing to be the door for God's love to walk through. So, I did what most millennials would do; I went on YouTube and began to search for people that operated or knew more about the gift. I saw names such as Clark Taylor, William Branham, Jason Chin, and then my godbrother would show me videos of Shawn Bolz, Dan Mohler, and Todd White. I do not know why I thought watching videos and reading about these guys would automatically allow me to operate like them. I did not realize that all of them relied on their connection with God. For you to be God's voice, you must trust Him. You must believe that He is speaking to you and telling you things that will help people.

I came across Jason Chin's videos; he was young and spoke about getting words of knowledge for people who needed healing. That was on a Monday; I said to myself Sunday, when I go to service, I'm not leaving without asking God to give me a word for someone in the congregation. Sunday came, and I was playing the bass guitar in church while my brother Willie was on the organ. Willie never became upset when I put the bass guitar down to focus on hearing from God. He is known for being a perfectionist, play the wrong note, and the death stare is coming next, hahaha. He is a phenomenal musician, and I have learned plenty from him. I am glad he allowed me to take that time out to focus. I would not be where I am as a prophet if Willie considered my playing more important.

During service that Sunday, I remember asking God to give me a word for someone. A word to help them understand that God is real, and He cares for them. While glancing at the congregation, I could not stop looking at this person. I thought it was me, but now I know it was God highlighting them in the crowd. He wanted me to go to that person and share what I heard concerning them. I now call it the "Eagle Eye," if you know me, I love referencing movies, so that is why I use metaphors or analogies. After I could not stop looking at them, I started to say to myself, God, what do I say to them? What started with sharing God's love with one person began to ignite a fire inside of me to share this gift every time I attended a worship service.

I started with only telling someone a couple of words, and then I grew to tell them a sentence. And then something happened to me; I started writing what I heard from God on my phone. I remember the first time, like yesterday. God highlighted someone at the worship service where I was playing drums. When the song was over, I started writing what I heard in my head for that person. I noticed I had written more than I have ever said face to face to a person. I was amazed because usually I would say a little phrase and say to myself, wow God, I know you are saying more than that, but you know what?

There were times where I was scared to say some things face to face because I didn't want to be wrong. But I felt comfortable when I wrote the words down. I trusted more of what I heard when I wrote the words down. I started writing the words that I heard for people and would go to them and show them my phone. And they would read it and say, "Wow, how did you know that?" I would say, "God told me." I realized that God was thinking about them and that they were on his mind. He

80

wanted them to know that He cared and that He was taking care of them. And God was using me to express that to them. There is an overwhelming feeling; knowing some stranger that doesn't know anything about you reveals a secret that only you and God knows and takes no credit for it, just so that you can believe with proof that God is real, that He knows, and loves you.

My goal was to help people. I knew the feeling of not knowing if God is real or not. I knew what it felt not to know if He was mad at you or if He loved you? Or if He was proud of you? Then someone shares what you have been thinking about and the questions you were asking yourself with no previous conversations. One night I was asleep, and I woke up around 5 am. I remember my parents always saying when they were awake, they would pray and ask God what He wanted them to know. What was He trying to reveal to them? So, I did the same thing, and a name came to my mind, and as soon as I focused on the name, I started hearing words for them. So, I grabbed my phone and started writing the words down.

"I was feeling in my heart that you were at a point that you were seeking God; your heart was searching after him. But then people started to hurt you, and pain came in. And most of these people were churchgoers, and because they are churchgoers, you started to take a step back because their actions lead to condemnation and judgment. Therefore, your portrait of God is blurry, and you do not know if He is real. Yes, you have been in church all your life, and you have heard about him, but no one told you that He loves you very much, and

He is not mad at you. He knows that your heart is searching for him, and He is waiting for you every time that you take the time to talk to Him, even if it is one word or one sentence. He has great plans for you, and He wants to use you. You have a great story to tell people, and you will lead many people to the Light of Jesus. For you do not know how much he loves you. I was sitting here praying, and you popped into my mind, so that means that God was thinking about you, and he wants all your needs met, and He wants you to feel His love."

This is the first time I woke up in the middle of the night and wrote words for someone. It was amazing. I did not even proofread it; I just wrote without seeing if it was true or not. I was scared to send it because I knew the individual, and they never received a message from me like that. I was battling with whether I should send it. I woke up the next day, and I could not shake it from my mind. I finally sent it and waited for a response. I was so nervous, but the person later sent something back and said just the night before they were ready to give up. They said everything was accurate, and after reading this, she will not give up!! I said, wow. God, wow, you are sooo good!

I did not want to stop now. I started to trust God more. Listen more. I remember one of my mentors Michael Kelley used to say all the time. Hear, trust, obey, no exceptions. I would hear him and ponder about it. Saying to myself, I wish that were easy for me. See, me growing up in the denomination that I was in, you hear about obedience all the time.

That word was a word I did not want to hear. But thank God for revealing to me some steps that needed to come before a person can obey.

This little equation came to me: Love + Trust = True Obedience.

I learned it's difficult to listen when you do not trust. A person can tell us, do not go down that road; it's a dead end. And if we don't know them or trust them, we will not listen, even if that person was right. I realized how many people will not obey God if they do not know how to hear his voice first. And then they will have to know he wants the best for them and has the best intentions for them. I believe once they see that He loves them and cares for them. They will trust Him, listen, and follow what He asks for them to do without hesitation. My kids first must know my voice and then recognize it; they must trust that it is in their best interest every time I tell them to do something. That is why we can't be selfish when we are asking our kids to do something. They will remember and begin to rebel because they know there is no benefit of what you ask them to do. God, our Father, does not say to himself; you are my children, so you better do what I want. No, everything we do has a purpose of helping us and someone else.

I love Romans 10:14-17 MSG. The Message version of the Bible says it best, "But how can people call for help if they don't know who to trust? And how can they know who to trust if they have not heard of the one who can be trusted? And how can they hear if nobody tells them? And how is anyone going to tell them unless someone is sent to do it?" When I learned this, I started to help people hear the voice of God and then help them to trust God. People began to take off in their journeys. So yes, knowing that God loves you and wants the best for you will convince you to listen, follow, and ask Him what He has for you to do. Hear, trust, and obey, as Michael said.

NOTES

Love of God Helped Me to Walk in My Gift

9

I love to make people happy, and I know I got that from my parents and through fellowship with the Holy Spirit, so I had a double whammy of it. I would love to see people happy after getting an encouraging word from God. I began by going to people privately after services or sending them a text message of the word I received. But never out in the open. Yes, I spoke and gave sermons, but I did not think about operating in that gift when I was up to speak. I always wanted to be prepared. To have an outline ready or some notes ready, so I did not mess up. I knew if I had an outline and notes, then I would always be safe. That all changed one day.

I was at a service, and I was playing my bass guitar, and the Pastor, William Kelley, got up and said, "God said Michael has a word for us." There were two Michaels there, my mentor and I. Michael was also a musician who plays the keyboard, I enjoyed playing bass guitar with him at his service; he would also take time to mentor me. At one of the services, Pastor William said he would call me the black Michael and call his son the white Michael. It cracked me up because he was a funny guy and deeply knowledgeable about God. Therefore, this service, when he said, "God said Michael has a word for us," I'm thinking, ok he's looking at me, but he means his son Michael, and then he pointed to me and said, "Yes, you Michael." I know everyone was shocked too. I was put on the spot and had no notes, no outlines of what I would do. I felt like that was the longest time frame ever in my life. I had to take my bass guitar off and walk to grab the mic. But you know what, as soon as I grabbed the mic, words began to come to me. I started sharing what was on my heart and ended with a testimony of me battling with panic attacks and how I overcame that situation.

When I ended, people came up and started singing and releasing things bothering them or negative thoughts, trying to control them. People thanked me for the transparency and the words that I was saying because they experienced something similar or something close to it. Then I realized that God does not want me to focus on my notes or my outline. You want to help people. You want me to push my agenda to the side and take on yours.

I will never forget William Kelley for that; his family called him Poppie, he was like a grandfather to me. He believed in me and allowed me to minister and encourage the people at his church. Poppie and I would sit down and talk for hours, laughing and him giving me advice. I was shocked. He was in his late 70s, early 80s, and he would allow me to speak in front of his service with no warning to the people. The people had never heard me say anything before except for when they greeted me after service. This situation is not common. Some people sit under a ministry for years and never get to say anything. The unique part was that I was not a member of their church; I was visiting at that time once a month to play for their Sunday Night worship service. I was a minister under my father, and as I said before, my father shared the podium. If you said you had a word, he let you speak. But this was uncommon in a lot of ministries. I am grateful for that opportunity; It taught me a lot, including confidence and boldness.

I was glad to be a musician because I was able to go to different ministries to play. And while I would visit, I would take a lot of notes. I would see the differences in the beliefs, or when many people are similar, and they never knew it. I have played at the charismatic churches where they are energetic and express themselves with singing, dancing, and shouting. I have also played at places where it was considered rude and interrupting the service if you made a noise. I played at a Seventh Day Adventist Church where a young preacher Myron Edmonds came in and helped the congregation not just go to a building but be the church that Christ wanted from us, which is to go outside the walls and show the love of God. I saw him suffer for it.

I saw people not wanting to change from their traditional teachings. It was encouraging because I was a young minister growing in the Love of God and seeing that I was accused of being too nice, too loving, and too forgiving. I also spoke about Grace and Love too much. What people never knew was I did not speak about Love, Grace, Mercy, and Forgiveness to dismiss holiness. I spoke about it because it is holiness! Seeing Myron struggle with helping people see from another perspective helped me realize that not everyone is open to new ideas and ways of looking at things. And that we all have our traditions and cultural influences that are hard to let go of.

I understand because there are things that were hard for me to let go. I am still open to learning what I am holding on to blocking my vision or hearing. Once I realized that I could learn from my, at the time 5-year-old, daughter Angelina, I said to myself, "You can learn from anyone." My daughter helped me to pray the way that I do now. I would have her pray at night before going to bed, and this time it was different. You know how a kid's favorite way of praying is, "Thank you, Jesus, for my mommy and daddy, my family, etc., it's always so special that it leaves parents and grandparents smiling and proud. Well, my daughter, this time, started to pray and say, "Thank you, Jesus, that my parents took me to Disneyland for my birthday and thank you, Jesus, that at my school we played this new game shark attack and I had fun." While hearing her pray, I wanted to stop her because I thought this is no way to pray, but I never stopped her, and then God showed me she was speaking to God like He is in the room. She was speaking to Him like He exists and is a real person. At times I think we forget that He is a person and that we can speak to Him and express how we feel at that very moment. I like the lyrics from Jesus Culture; Kim Walker sang, "I don't want to talk about you like you're not in the room, I want to look right at you, I want to sing right to you." That is what my daughter was doing; she was talking right to Him. And that is what changed the way I communicate with God.

I would go around interviewing people, asking people what they thought about certain topics. I knew if I wanted to help people, I needed to know what people were looking for and what people thought about their relationship with God. As I received answers from different individuals, I began to ponder on their responses. I would pray and complete my spiritual practices to hear from God. I wanted practical examples and relative analogies to help paint a picture. I tried to help as many people as I could. I knew at that time a lot of churchgoers were not transparent. They struggled with answering questions. I remember hearing the older generation say whatever they heard; they did not question it; they just went with it. So, when the younger generation grew up and asked questions, the older generation looked at it as rebellion or not humbled. The older generation did not realize that asking questions is being humble. If you ask someone a question, you are saying I don't know everything, and I would love for you to help me with the information I do not know. Some of the older generations did not take the time to ponder what they were hearing and the things they felt. If they did, some would not have struggled with being asked questions or thinking individuals were questioning, leaving the faith, or dismissing their spirituality.

My drive was in helping people, being around people. I would talk on the phone for hours, helping people see how much God loves them and sharing spiritual practices I used to help me grow spiritually. I knew if it worked for me, then it would work for them. Everything I was involved in began to change because I would bring a different perspective. For our gospel group Nu Covenant to grow up in the same denomination and upbringing, we all believed the same way. For me, to let them know not to focus on how much we love God, but for us to focus on how much He loves us was different. I told them about my experience at worship service where everyone in the building was standing and singing; it was awesome. I was also participating by raising my hands and just singing the songs the worship team was singing. They were singing, "Jesus, we love you." I immediately asked the question, "God, do you hear us? Do you know how much we love you?" and I heard God speak back and say, "I do hear you; I do know how much you all love me, but that's not the problem. The problem is you all don't know how much I love you." I started to cry after I heard those words because that is why we find ourselves broken, insecure, and in need of validation. After all, we do not know that the Father of perfect love wants us. He wants to be in our lives. Let me repeat it; He wants to be in our lives.

I feel that most people would say, "God, I love you," because they were afraid if they don't say those words, then God will be mad at them and not want anything to do with them. Actually, God knows that you need first to know that He loves you, how can you show love when

94

you do not know anything about it? How can you say you love if no one ever showed you what love is? Yet the Father knowing comes and loves on you, showing you goodness and kindness so you can understand how to show that to someone else. A person that genuinely loves doesn't care about what someone is doing to them; they can't stop showing love because that's who they are, that's because it's real. If you genuinely love your child, it doesn't matter what he/she does or if he/she listens to you or not, you still find ways to help your child. You still find ways to give them a better future. You share your heart with them: that you love them, why you want them to listen to you, and the benefits of listening to what you've told them to do. Their behavior does not change your love for them. Right? When kids are not listening, I do not think you say, "You are making me not love you anymore." That does not sound right. So, imagine how much your behavior is not changing the way God is feeling about you.

My group, Nu Covenant, helped me move forward in a lot of areas. We were able to sing in many places, and because some of the leaders who oversaw the events were believers in the move of God, they would ask us not to hold back. If we wanted to pray for people or give encouraging words, we were told to do so. I remember the first time I stopped singing and went to pray for someone in the crowd. I would operate like this when I was by myself or at a service, but I never did it with my singing group. This time my heart was open, and when we were given permission before service, I did not hold back. We were at this youth event called Summerfest, invited by our friend Israel Cintron. It was our first time singing there. There was a huge crowd of young people that loved God. We began to sing, the atmosphere changed, and you could see people beginning to open their hearts and receive. I went into the crowd and started to pray for people there. This was different because we are a group that likes to sing harmony, and if I do not have the mic, then the harmony will be off. That was not my concern, I could feel the hearts of the people there, and I wanted to help. That day helped our group to see that, yes, we were singing, but most importantly, we were ministering to the needs of the people.

So, one day, I pushed myself to the limit. I knew our group was invited to sing in Erie, PA. I was at home in my room listening to this worship instrumental by my friend Bo Salisbury. I was asking God to reveal to me the names of who would be at the event. I saw Shawn Bolz do this a lot, so I knew I could try to see if it worked for me too. I also wanted to hear a word for the ministry and the ministry leaders that would be present. As I was listening for names, I wrote down a woman's name, and when I wrote down her name on my phone, words came to me concerning her.

"You have been praying for your kids, and it seems like your prayers are not getting anywhere. But God hears them. And he is coming to your rescue. A promotion or new job is coming your way too, so your finances can increase."

"You have been struggling financially for years, and this is the end of that. You will begin to see an increase in every area of your life."

"Your husband was hurt on his job and was relying on you to bring finances in. The struggle is over. I release increase right now!!"

Those are the words that came to me for her. Now, remember I am at home in the room by myself. So, I know I received those words, but I did not know if it was accurate. I just kept it and waited for the day of the event. I received this word in August, and the concert was in October, so it stayed in my mind building up to the event. I heard words for the ministry and some other people connected to the ministry, but the main concern was who this woman was? Will she be at the concert? Are these words for her?

October 6th came, and our singing group drove to the concert. They did not know that I would get up and say the words I was hearing or even call out the names I received at home. The concert started a little later because of traveling difficulties with the other groups on the program; it prevented me from giving the word while our group was singing, but I asked the MC if I could give the words I received. I started with the ministry leaders, and then I said to myself, there isn't enough time. I will ask if these other names I call are here, then to please come to me after service, and I will reveal what I received. When the service ended, I went to our merchandise table to greet the people there, and then a lady came to me and said, do you have a message for me? You called out my name during service. And I said, "Oh wow, yes." I gave her my phone with the words on it and told her to see if it makes sense. She looked at me with big eyes and said, "Wait, how do you know this? This is all true." I looked at her with a shocked look on my face too, and I said, "This was all God; he gave me your name, and the words followed."

She then told me, "I don't live here, I live in New York, and I was thinking of not coming to this concert, but I wanted to see my family here." That is when my mind was blown. Just think about it, I received that word for her two months before the concert. And that shows that God put it on her heart to come to the concert knowing that he had an on-time word for her. Wow! She and I both were shocked, and she asked, "Are you some kind of a prophet?" and I said to her, "I'm just a believer." The other leaders from that ministry confirmed the things I said for them, and that's when I said to myself, "I need to keep pushing and make sure I call my friend Bo and say awesome worship instrumental, it's a sign that it will accomplish what you created it to do."

What gifts do you feel God pulling your heart towards using?

What are your fears about using these gifts?

If you choose not to use your gifts, what will your community/ministry be missing?

NOTES

The Community That Helped
Sharpen My Gifts

10

I will encourage you to get around people. You will learn a lot about yourself. You will also see yourself being less judgmental as well. The more you surround yourself with people and allow them to speak, the more you will understand and not assume. I thank God for the opportunity to volunteer for the Rape Crisis Center. A lady named Shelley Hunt was the Director of Victim Services and a member at the service I played guitar for. I spoke with her and shadowed her to learn more about what she does. I later decided to participate in training for the text line advocate. I would work the late-night shift 12 am – 6 am because having three daughters made it difficult to complete any daytime shifts. It was required for volunteers to have 20 hours a month, and the day shifts were only 2-hour blocks; the only long block was the night shift for 6 hrs. I worked the six-hour shift once a week to meet the requirements. I would chat with individuals that were feeling anxiety or discomfort about their past experiences. Some woke up from a nightmare reimagining their events. Or even people that could not go to sleep because of trauma. I also spoke to parents that were looking for advice for their kids that experienced abuse. I did this for six months. I heard a lot of stories, and there were times where I wanted to cry. I said to myself, I need to be more understanding of those around me. Volunteering was extremely hard for me. Being a minister and a teacher of Love and God, I was used to giving spiritual advice. I was used to helping people apply spiritual practices to help with personal issues, but I could not say anything about God; I couldn't give spiritual advice. All I could do was listen and try to comfort them without beliefs and personal opinions. Nevertheless, I needed these experiences and after this experience, I said to myself, everyone in ministry should volunteer. We should all know how to listen to people's stories and not be quick to judge and know when people are just trying to vent. What they need from us is to be an ear and allow them to voice it.

Now I would recommend the night shift because it is so quiet and still an excellent opportunity to pray and worship. I even had an awesome experience that I would never forget; it was 4:56 am, and no one was on the chat. I only had an hour left of the shift, and most of the time around this time, I would not get any more chats. So, as I was sitting there praying, my new friend Tom came to my mind, and I began to write the words I heard for him. Now I met Tom through my brother Marc, they have sung together in a group called Radiate Live. Tom is also a producer and was helping our group Nu Covenant on a project. I would visit his home a few times to fill in for Marc or help with the Nu Covenants project. I did not know much about him except that he was married, and he had a very hyper dog. Thank God he would always put the dog in the garage when I came over. To hear words concerning him was a little strange because I was not thinking of him, but I just wrote whatever came to me. And here it is what I received.

"You have been having questions about God. You are interested. You want to know, what is the hype? You want to see what everyone has been talking about. "You and your wife have been struggling to have kids. Having the dog helps you both cope with the problem. It hurts you, but you try to avoid it as much as possible.

"God the Father wants to heal you both. Naturally and spiritually. You both have amazing hearts, but yours stick out the most. Many people look up to you

104

because you are a leader, and when you speak, an atmosphere follows you. You want to change the world either with music or "book" - I do not know if you write or want to.

"God loves you, and he is protecting you right now. I know those panic attacks try to take over you, but his love is coming right now to take it away. His love is coming to make sure you don't experience that again."

I was so scared to tell him because this word was precise. There were no grey areas in this. They either have been trying to have kids or not. I did not want him to say, "Now I know God is not real because that's not true." So, I kept the word from him. Do you know I went to his house two times, saw his wife the first time, and did not say anything and did not say anything the second time as well? Now the third time I went over there, he started to ask about my kids, and then I said, "I can't hold this anymore although I wrote the message almost a month ago, I have to show you. Let me know if it makes sense or not."

He read the message and looked at me, and said, "Wait, let me read that again." He said, "There is no way I told you, and I know I haven't told your brother. We only told two people who couldn't have said anything to you." Then he told me that the same day after I wrote that message at 4:56 am, his wife took a pregnancy test and found out she was pregnant. God is sooo good!! God took care of their situation. He and I both were shocked! I know I heard that word and felt power when writing it down, but I was nervous. You know, once the meditation, prayer, or worship is over, your human mind begins to doubt what you heard in the secret place.

I remember going to CVS, and he called me saying, "Michael, what should I do now?" He wanted to know if God wanted him to do something. I could tell he was trying to understand what was going on, especially when you hear so many different things about God. For a lot of us, our first response when we see that God has our attention is, "God, what do you want me to do?" I told him to listen to a few songs I recommended. I encouraged him to allow those songs to minister to him. One of the songs was titled "Pieces" by Stephany Gretzinger and Amanda Cook from Bethel. The song spoke to me about the true character of God and how he does not give his heart in pieces and that he does not hide himself to tease us. The song also had a spontaneous worship part where she was singing and saying things from her heart that helped us see the nature of God. I learned that we do not always have to run someone straight to the Bible to help introduce them to God. We can use something familiar to them to help minister the gospel. Knowing how much he loves music and singers could open the door to help him understand the heart of God. He could learn that God was a father. A loving Father at that. A Father that wants to heal and answer prayers. A Father that comes to our rescue when we are stuck and have no way to escape. I could tell he was shocked when I told him to listen to these songs because it seemed so simple, but I knew God was going to visit him when he started listening to those songs. And guess what, he did. Tom now sends me songs that are encouraging and reveal the heart of God, and now he has a healthy baby boy.

Therefore, I say God is a good Father because He loves to help people. He needs someone that will not stay silent but will speak out a word into the atmosphere that will manifest. It is amazing because I have met a lot of prophets that would do just that. Speak out a word, and that day or very soon, I or the people in the congregation received just what they said. I had the opportunity to play for a Prophet named Israel Ford, and when he would speak, he would take time out to prophesy and speak about what was going to happen to the people that week or that month. And there were times when he spoke; I saw that word come true in my life. I witnessed him combine prophesying with speaking from his original sermon. I thought it was awesome because it was encouraging to the people, and people need to see more than the scriptures; they need to see the scriptures come alive by signs and right-now miracles. I started to include prophesying in my messages; I heard what God said to the whole congregation and spoke it out. Another Pastor, Allen Rasnake, gave me advice and said, "Hey, if you're feeling in your heart that there are people in the audience feeling guilty or feeling depressed. You don't have to call them forward, but you can speak forth a word to the congregation, and they will receive it while in their seats.

One day Pastor Michael Kelley, whom I was playing bass for every Sunday night, came to me and said he wanted me to give the exhortation before offering every Sunday night. I was so thrilled; I could not wait to tell my wife that I had a 10-minute window to encourage the people. My position was to encourage people to give money, but most importantly, why we asked them to give money. I learned that God gave to us freely, and if he owns everything, what material or monetary gift could we give to Him? Nothing, right? I realized that we could show God gratitude and thanks by giving, so someone else can have. I found stories or analogies to motivate people to give for that cause. I was happy to know that the money was helping the people in need, so I was confident in speaking about it. I would not have taken that role if I felt no one was being helped. Every Sunday night, I would get up and encourage the people. I remember one day, my wife said to me, "Awesome stories, and the people are receiving it, but you should put in a 'thank you to the people." And I said, "Wow, you're right, honey." There is an appreciation in saying thank you. I did the offering exhortation for years. I loved that more than playing my bass guitar. There was a sense of gratefulness and encouragement I felt being able to encourage others. Most of my stories were everyday life situations that I had experienced or revelations I was giving that helped them see from another perspective. It was awesome, and the more comfortable I became, I began to start prophesying and speaking into the atmosphere for people and their situations. Every Sunday night, I would get excited driving an hour there, many of the times praying on the way there and praying coming home.

I continued the offering exhortation at New Life Ministries, and when they merged with Trinity Gospel Temple, I was learning something that I wanted to take back to my Father's Ministry at Greater Fair Temple. People want to know where their money is going. People would like it better if you told them the church bills are this much money, and we need your support to help pay it. When we try to use fear to motivate people to give, it will never work; you will always see less giving. But when people see that God loves them so much that He will take care of their needs, they realize it is a privilege to help the ministry and the people connected to it. People will give. Just be honest with people, and the more they realize they are blessed and have more than enough, they will give so much more where all the ministry's needs are met.

A lot of people gave me advice and helped me grow into the person I am today. The experiences have helped me to love people and be more understanding of people's needs. That is what I saw in the life of Jesus; He always took care of the people's needs. There are many times in the scriptures where we see that. So, not only can our money help people, but our time, effort, and most importantly, our words. I hear many people say today, "people are so sensitive," to try to convince themselves why it's ok to be mean. We all can be honest with no judgment attached, with no hypocrisy attached. When Jesus told the people, "Whoever is without sin, throw the first stone," he was trying to get them to see there was no difference in what the lady did and what they have done. It is hard for us to see we all are in the same boat. It is hard for us to understand or look from another perspective.

Many people would talk about people who have sex outside of marriage but never thought they would do the same thing if it were easier to complete the task? For example, if someone called their boyfriend over for a night of Netflix and chill and something else also happens that night, people would talk about them harshly. But the question is if they had the same opportunity, would they turn it down? If someone came over unannounced and threw themselves on them, would they deny it? See, that becomes a little harder. I learned if we were put in other people's predicament, some of us would make the same decision, and that's ok; that's why we are allowing the Love of God to transform us to be more than enough. Some will get there faster than others, but you cannot say at 100 years old, "Why are people fornicating? I'm not doing that." Yeah, of course, you are not.

I had many opportunities to show the Love of God to people, whether it was giving them words from God, encouraging them with analogies and stories, or helping them not to worry. Or giving money away for no reason. I would get paid every Sunday and find someone to give money to. I remember going to this gas station every Sunday night and waiting to see how much money people were putting towards gas. If it were less than $20, I would give the clerk money to help that person. The clerk and I became friends; he knew that I was looking for someone to help when he saw me on Sunday. Someone came in with $2 asking for gas, and he looked straight at me, knowing that we found someone to help. He never knew I was coming from service until one day, he asked. I am glad he did not know because I wanted him to see that I was a regular person, no different than him that desired to help people. See, when someone sees you dressed just like them and you show the love of God, it stays on their mind. Some people are not used to experiencing people giving away money or helping people they do not know. So, when they see this, they are intrigued to know who you are, and they want to listen to what you have to say. I made God more famous every Sunday night.

I am grateful for my experiences. I am also thankful for everyone that has helped me become who I am today. If I name everyone that ever helped me, the book will never end. Many have called me with encouraging words or prophesied to me. Texted me, gave me money without asking me if I needed it. I want to thank all of you from my heart. Remember the times you and I connected! Please know it helped me move to the next level. It was hard writing this book because of the battle of not feeling good enough or not being qualified. I realized that we all have a story, and one person's life can change by hearing your story. I have been writing to a friend that I met in prison while ministering there. He and I connected right away. He could tell I was a believer in the Love of God and that I do not believe in behavior modification but heart transformation. I do struggle with reaching out to the people I care about. One of the reasons is because I am shy, private, and stay to myself. I am not outspoken, but God has been helping me with that.

When I met Ja'Relle Smith in prison and gave him my email, I thought I wouldn't hear from him until he was released from jail, but no, he wrote to me the following week. I was thrilled to speak to him because of how humble he was. I could tell he knew more scriptures than I. I found out he knew where to find them as well. But what stood out was that he was not arrogant. He asked for my view and perspective on a lot of topics. We would go back and forth, giving words of knowledge to each other, and we would also prophesy. I told him that I saw him released from prison, and we emailed back and forth until it happened.

Ja'Relle helped me see that our family and friends and even the people we do not know need us. They need us to be there for them to reach out. Take the time to message them back or call them back to speak to them on the phone. Our family lost a person that we loved and cared for to suicide. He was important to our family. At times we blame ourselves for the lack of communication or if we missed the signs. My brothers and I called him Uncle Mark; he loved our singing group. He wanted to do any and everything for us to be known all over the world. He was so proud to call us nephews. He was my father's best friend from the Navy, and they never gave up their friendship. My father considered him a brother. It hurt him and our family to lose him. We wished we could speak to him and let him know that we were there for him and that no matter how hard it got, he had us rooting for him.

My godbrother Ricardo was in jail for ten years, and not once did I reach out to say, brother, I am here for you. I felt terrible about that later, and now having Ja'Relle as a friend, I told myself I would do better. Not only did I message him, but I found more people to message, encourage, and build up. I kept reminding myself, how can I say I am too busy to write them when I experience the freedom to wake up when I want, to go to sleep when I want. To work when I want. The least I can do is take some time out of my day to encourage them and even listen to them. You'd be surprised that they don't like the spotlight to be on themselves. Most care more about your day, what you're doing, and encouraging you to keep your head up. Crazy right?

So many encouraged me to write a book, and now I finally did. I remember going out of town to a worship conference in Maryland, where I experienced amazing things. God showed off during those three days! One night as I was there, Pastor David Whittington told everyone to touch their neighbors and pray for them. So, a lady sitting next to me put her hand on my arm, and then I felt someone put their hand on my back. So, the lady next to me prayed and took her hand away, but the person behind me kept their hand on my back, so I knew they were not finished praying. As time went on, I thought to myself, "wow, they are praying for a long time." I started to look out of my peripheral, but I didn't see anyone. But I still felt a hand on my back. So now I am thinking, "wait, what is going on" so I turned around, and no one was there. I immediately knew an angel was touching my back! It was amazing. I had a lot of encounters at that conference, mind-blowing encounters! I also saw a vision for the ministry that the Pastors let me reveal to the congregation, and when I finished telling them what I saw from God, they thanked me for my heart and prayed for me, and even spoke amazing things in my life that came to pass.

I was in tears by how much Grace was released to me in that place. People took turns prophesying and releasing what they heard from God for me. I remember when service was over, people in the audience had words of knowledge for me. It was a mind-blowing experience. For instance, I met Bernadette Cole, who encouraged me to continue writing this very book. She helped me understand how angels communicate and said she'd seen me writing in a red notebook. She couldn't have known that my notebook would be this book, but it was just the push I needed to keep from quitting.

I knew there was something special when I wrote things down, but I never understood why until I met Pastor Brian Timberlake. I met him at his Church Anniversary, where one of my friends, William Beasley, asked me to play bass guitar there. It was a 3-night Anniversary celebration, but I could only play for the 1st and 3rd nights. The first night I went there, I had a good time playing, and I also saw Pastor Timberlake giving words of knowledge to some people in the crowd. I was intrigued because he did not need to write the words he was getting on a phone or on paper to give to people as I did. The night ended, and the only thing Pastor Timberlake said to me was, "Thank you so much for playing; we appreciate it," and he paid me. I missed the second night and came back the third night to play, but this time something happened after the praise team finished. I saw a vision of Pastor Timberlake writing at a desk, and then words started to come to me. I knew I needed to go to the back to write it down, so I went to the back and began to write what I was hearing for him. A long time ago, I would have never approached Pastors, Ministers, or other Speakers present. A lady I met at a radio station spoke to me and said, "When God gives you a word for people that you think are in a high position, don't be afraid to voice it; speak what you hear." Since I heard that, I did not hold back, even when I heard words for guest speakers. I gave them the words I heard for them. That night I began to write what I was hearing and seeing.

> "I saw you receive many blessings because of the words you spoke in the atmosphere. You are constantly speaking things to existence and planting seeds. I saw this huge field, and it represents all the seeds you planted".

"You're not afraid to speak when there is something new and good happening for someone around you. And sometimes you may say to yourself, 'Should I say that?'. You think to yourself; it is like I am always saying that a blessing is coming, or things that people need are coming! But what is happening is that the Father is using your faith to operate in others' lives. When you speak out the word, the angels grab that word and begin to work in those people's lives. And those lives are being changed. Plenty is happening in your field; you will see a financial increase. You will see those needs met. You will experience abundance because of those words spoken in the lives of others.

> "I see you were writing on this paper ... I do not know what that means, but I know there is more the father is going to reveal to you. Things that you and your wife have been pondering and thinking about. Even those things that you

114

worry about, I see you up at night praying, know the father sees you and he is coming. I even smiled writing that part because I can feel the love and the joy of God for you, Brother."

I wrote this down in the back of the building near the restroom, and I went back into the service. I signaled for William and told him I had a word that I needed to share. William texted the Pastor and asked could I reveal it, and Pastor Timberlake said I could. I was shocked he said yes. I have experienced pastors denying me an opportunity to speak. To have Pastors allow me to share what I was feeling is awesome. Close to the end of service, I was asked by the Pastor to reveal this word, and after I finished, Pastor Timberlake looked at me and said, "Man of God, thank you for that, that word was sincere; and it saved my life."

Immediately I started crying because, to be honest, I am just trying to hear from God. And I want to help people. It does not matter how many times I give a word to someone; it always gives me joy when I hear someone tell me that God is thinking about me and what future things are in store—or even making known to me things I discuss with God in my time. After that, Pastor Timberlake started confirming some of the things I was saying. And he did not have to do that. He could have said thank you and moved on, but no, he was very transparent with everyone about how he felt. And then he turned to me and started to prophesy to me and speak some things in my life, and I started crying again.

After service, we spoke, and he encouraged me to keep speaking and not to hold back. We exchanged numbers, and one day we were checking on each other, and he found out I was speaking at my home church. So, he came, and while I was up to speak, I had some names that came to me while I was praying at home the night before. So, I gave those people the words I heard for them and then spoke my message. Later that day, Pastor Timberlake and I spoke on the phone, and he revealed to me something that I have been asking for years, "Why is it so easy for me to operate in the prophetic by writing words down on my phone or paper for people?" I told him how I wish I were more like him and how he did not need a paper; he was hearing and speaking. Then he tells me that I am a Prophetic Scribe; I had never even heard about that. I started researching Prophetic Scribes and realized, wow, that does sound like me. A couple of signs that may show that you are a prophetic scribe according to (The Chamber of the Scribe) by Theresa Harvard Johnson:

- They write or record from a strong, unplanned, or unrehearsed flow.
- The words simply stream from the spirit of the Lord into their hearing and through their recording device or pen. This includes dialogue, novel scenes, songs, poetry, spoken word, the wording of letters, etc.
- Prophetic Scribes also have a pre-occupation with recording what they see, hear, and/or experience from God.
- As the gift matures, they begin to experience a desire to share what they receive with others.
- They may have a special gift and anointing to hear and see stories, articles, novels, and books in the loves of or on behalf of others.

- They walk under a special grace in which they are primarily "recorders" in the Kingdom.

These are just a couple of signs of a Prophetic Scribe. On the Chamber of the Scribe website, you can find more signs. There is an article sharing 26 signs of a Prophetic Scribe. Thank God for this site because now I have accepted who I am, and it helped me flow more and not to fight the feeling to write down what I see and hear. And because of this, I have helped a lot of people. I have helped people to see that God is thinking of them by sharing their private prayers or things on their minds. I have spoken that miracle money was coming, promotions on their jobs, or even raises. I operate in more boldness, knowing who I am and what my God-given abilities are. This helped with confidence in sharing the words I hear with Pastors, Prophets, Musicians, and many more. Some believers have opened their hearts to listen to what I had to say, and most of the time, it shocked me.

Remember, I am known more as a musician and a singer in the group Nu Covenant. And most musicians are not taken seriously. There are times where the musician can feel the shift in the atmosphere or hear words from God and is never given a chance to share. The audience often saw me on my bass guitar, and then after service, I am giving people in the audience words that I heard while service was going on.

I was playing the drums and bass guitar while someone was speaking to the congregation. I heard words concerning her and her family and the things she had been praying for. I was so scared to say something because I knew she was just the speaker of that night, and she knew that I was the musician for that night. So, all I did was give her my phone and said: "these were the words I heard for you." I was shocked to hear that the words were accurate. She had a shocked look on her face as well, probably thinking, I know there wasn't another pastor or prophet here that introduced themselves, and I know he was the musician of the night, but how did he know that?

I want to encourage the musicians reading this that just because you are gifted to play does not mean you cannot operate in the prophetic. And yes, can we prophesy with our instrument, but we can also prophesy with our lips and pens. I want to thank everyone that encouraged me to play and to speak. Those are the kind of people you need in your life. People that do not put limitations on you. Someone that looks at you and says, "I see more for you." I see you operating in more of the gifts of the spirit.

I always thought that the things that happened to me were weird, and now I see that Todd Dulaney says it best, "Through all I have been through, it was God pulling me through." Just remember that God the Father loves you and if you want to know more about Him, get in His presence which will reveal His heart and the way He feels about you. I am a true believer in letting His presence tell you who He is. I love you all and thank you for the opportunity to share my heart.

NOTES

Made in the USA
Middletown, DE
01 March 2022